INCREDIBLE CRIMES

INCREDIBLE CRIMES

BY LINDA ATKINSON

Franklin Watts
New York/London/Sydney/Toronto/1980
A Triumph Book

Photographs courtesy of:
United Press International: pp. 7, 16, 27, 63;
Wide World Photos: pp. 42, 46, 76, 85.

Headlines on page 67 © 1904/05 by
The New York Times Company. Reprinted by permission.

Library of Congress Cataloging in Publication Data

Atkinson, Linda.
Incredible crimes.

(A Triumph book)
Includes index.
SUMMARY: Relates five notorious crimes, including
D. B. Cooper's skyjacking, the great train robbery,
and the Krupp diamond case.
1. Crime and criminals—Case studies—
Juvenile literature. [1. Crime and criminals] I. Title.
HV6030.A85   364.1'552   80-12955
ISBN 0-531-04170-0

R. L. 2.5 Spache Revised Formula

CONTENTS

THE $200,000 SKY THEFT

"Name, please," the clerk said.

"D. B. Cooper," answered the man.

The clerk wrote it down. Then he gave Mr. Cooper his ticket.

"Next, please," said the clerk.

D. B. Cooper picked up his small brown suitcase. He walked quietly onto the runway and up the ramp to the aircraft.

"He was just another name on the list," the clerk would say later. "A plain, quiet man. There was nothing special about him."

Two stewardesses, Tina Mucklow and Florence Shaffner, were at the door of the plane. They smiled at Cooper as he came on board. He smiled back. He was no different from any of the other people getting on board. As the clerk said, there was "nothing special" about him. At least, not yet.

There was nothing special about the plane trip either. It was only a short run, a twenty-five-minute flight from Portland, Oregon, to Seattle, Washington.

"It was a humdrum flight," Shaffner said later. "I'd made it many times. The only thing that made this one a little special was the fact that it was Thanksgiving. Many of the people were going home for the holiday. Some of them were not used to flying. They were excited. And a little nervous."

Mr. Cooper wasn't nervous at all. At least, he didn't seem nervous. He stayed in his seat. He didn't say anything to anyone. He was quiet and calm.

Soon the doors closed. The "No Smoking" sign went on, then the sign which said, "Fasten your seat belts." And then the plane, a Boeing 727, took off.

Shaffner and Mucklow went to their station in the front of the plane. They began to prepare coffee for the passengers. From time to time, they checked the buttons on the wall. A flashing button was a signal that a passenger needed help.

Soon button number 25 flashed on.

"I'll go," Shaffner said.

She walked quickly down the aisle to seat 25. D. B. Cooper smiled up at her.

"Yes, sir," Shaffner said.

Cooper didn't answer. Instead, he handed the stewardess a note. She read it, and then stumbled back a step.

"I want $200,000," the note said, "in $20 bills. And I want two sport parachutes. Tell the Captain to get them. Now. If he doesn't, these will go off."

Shaffner looked at the man and gulped. He had snapped open his suitcase. Inside were two red cylinders. Attached to them were two coils of wire.

Shaffner had no idea whether or not the "bombs" were real. But she wasn't going to take any chances. She nodded to Cooper.

He grabbed the note back and stuffed it into his pocket.

Shaffner hurried to the cockpit.

"Oh, my God," Captain Scott said when Shaffner told him what had happened. "Did he seem wild? Did he seem crazy?"

"He was very calm, Captain," Shaffner said. "I think he knows exactly what he's doing."

"OK, let's get Seattle on the radio," the captain said, "and see what they think down there."

Quickly, he called the Seattle control tower.

"Hang on," the operator said. "I'll get Mr. Nyrop."

Sounds of static from the radio set filled the air. Then the voice of Don Nyrop, president of Northwest Airlines, came on.

"Tell him that we will do whatever he asks," Nyrop said. "This is on the level. Tell him we're rounding up the money and the parachutes right now. We'll let you know as soon as we have them. And Captain," he added, "good luck."

The captain turned to Shaffner.

"OK Florence," he said. "Tell Cooper what Nyrop said. Ask him what he wants us to do next."

The young woman hurried out of the cockpit and down the aisle. Within minutes, she was back.

"He says to keep circling until everything is ready," she said. "Then, he'll let us land."

The captain nodded.

"So far, so good then," he said. "Now let's think of something to tell the passengers."

He turned to the plane's loudspeaker system. "Ladies and gentlemen," he said, "this is the captain speaking. We are approaching the Seattle airport. But we are having trouble with our landing gear, and our landing will be delayed." Captain Scott cleared his throat. Then he went on. "There is no cause for alarm. Please stay in your seats and obey the 'No Smoking' sign. Thank you."

Soon the passengers could see the lights of the city below them. They put away their books and newspapers. They stretched and slipped into sweaters and shoes. They had all taken the captain at his word. They expected to land within minutes.

Shaffner and Mucklow walked up and down the aisle. They did not show how frightened they were. They smiled and chatted with the passengers. Except for the passenger in seat 25, this was still just a normal, "humdrum" flight. Everyone was, or seemed to be, calm.

But on the ground, things were far from calm. Dozens of people—from Northwest Airlines, from the police, from the FBI—were racing into Seattle to get the money Cooper had demanded. They couldn't get it all from the same bank. No bank had ten thousand $20 bills on hand!

Other people were trying to find the "sport" parachutes Cooper had demanded. Sport parachutes are the kind sky divers use. Airport workers were calling all the skydiving clubs in the area. But so far, no chutes had been found.

At the same time, the police and the FBI were trying to figure out who "D. B. Cooper" really was. But they had nothing to go on. He was

A man who called himself D. B. Cooper hijacked a jetliner flying over Washington State in 1971. He parachuted out of the aircraft with $200,000 ransom, and was never seen again.

just a name on the passenger list. Even the clerk who sold him his ticket could barely remember what he looked like.

The plane continued to circle the air above the field. An hour passed. The passengers were restless. Some of them were getting worried.

Finally, the captain called Shaffner to the cockpit. Nyrop was on the radio. He had good news.

"The money is ready," the president said. "Tell Cooper that. We've got it all—ten thousand $20 bills. It's his the minute you land."

"And the parachutes?" Captain Scott asked.

"No go, Captain. We haven't been able to get them. Tell Cooper we're doing our best, but sport chutes are hard to find. We've got regular chutes. Ask him if that's OK."

"You heard it," the captain said to Shaffner. "See how Cooper takes it."

Florence took a deep breath before she opened the cockpit door. Then, smiling "as usual," she walked quickly down the aisle. She knew that the passengers were watching her. She had to remain calm.

"Besides, in my heart," she said later, "I believed that it was over. I thought that the money would be enough, and that Cooper would say we could land."

She was wrong.

"Nothing doing," Cooper said when she gave him the message. "Get the chutes. Then we'll see."

Shaffner walked back to the cockpit. She was not so calm or hopeful now.

Captain Scott got back on the radio.

"No go, control," he said. "He won't take plain chutes. We'll have to continue circling."

A few minutes later, Shaffner came back to the cockpit.

"He's getting nervous, Captain," she said. "It doesn't look good. Isn't there any way they can rush things along?"

Captain Scott turned to the radio again.

"The guy is getting restless," he said. "Please advise."

"Impress on him," Nyrop said, "that we're not trying to stall. Tell him we are doing the best we can, as fast as we can. We are on the level. Tell him we'll talk directly to him if he wants."

[9]

Captain Scott was back on the radio within minutes.

"He doesn't want to talk," he said to the tower. "And he's getting scared. I don't like it. You've got to come up with the sport chutes quick."

The plane circled for another half an hour. Then Nyrop called back. The money and the chutes were ready and waiting.

Shaffner hurried up the aisle to give Cooper the news. Then she returned to the cockpit.

"He says we can land now, Captain," she said. "And he will let the passengers go as soon as he's checked the money and the parachutes."

Captain Scott turned to the loudspeaker again.

"Ladies and gentlemen," he said. "This is the captain speaking. We are about to land. But do not, I repeat, *do not* leave your seats even after we have landed. You will be told why once we are on the ground. I repeat, remain in your seats and wait for word from me."

The plane glided smoothly down. The engines were turned off. The passengers were worried and frightened. But they did not move.

Soon the captain came out of the cockpit. He walked down the aisle to seat 25. There he stopped.

"Ladies and gentlemen," he said. "May I have your attention. We are hostages," the captain said quickly, "of this man. He has asked for certain things. The airline has delivered them. He will let you all go as soon as they are delivered."

The passengers were silent. If they had any questions, they didn't ask them. They looked from Cooper to the captain and back again.

"All we could do was wait," one of them said later, "and hope that that man Cooper would be given whatever he wanted."

Soon a car pulled up beside the plane. Two men got out. One carried a sack of money. The other carried the parachutes.

The men walked up the ramp. They put their packages down at the door of the plane. Then they backed away.

The captain brought the packages inside. Cooper opened them. Everything was in order.

"That's it, Captain," he said. "They can go."

Policemen and FBI agents lined the airfield. But no one moved as the passengers filed out of the plane and down the ramp. Then the doors closed behind them. The engines roared. And with Cooper and the flight crew still on board, the giant 727 was in the air again. First it headed south. Then it changed course and began to head west.

The people on the ground were puzzled. They couldn't understand where Cooper was taking the plane. But they knew this much: it would need a landing strip of at least a mile (1.6 km) to come down on. And, it couldn't go very far without more fuel.

Airline workers checked maps of the area. They placed flags on the airstrips where they thought the plane could land. They called the local airports and asked them to report in—if and when the plane was spotted.

Meanwhile, the police and the FBI were talking to the passengers. Did any of them have any idea of what Cooper was up to? They didn't. They hadn't heard anything. They hadn't seen anything.

The FBI tried to work it out for themselves. Again and again, they wondered about the parachutes. Was Cooper really planning to jump? How could he? There were snowstorms all over the area. And the temperature was close to zero ($-18°$ C). What could Cooper have in mind?

On the aircraft, the crew was puzzled too. For a long time, Cooper didn't say anything. He just sat in his seat, looking out the window.

Finally, he called Tina Mucklow to his side.

"Tell the captain," he said in a low voice, "to go to Mexico."

Mucklow hurried down the aisle. A few minutes later, she was back.

"I'm sorry, sir," she said. "The captain says we don't have enough fuel to get to Mexico. You are welcome to come to the cockpit and see for yourself."

Cooper was thoughtful for a moment. Then he spoke.

"OK," he said, "OK. Tell the captain to head for Reno. We'll refuel there."

Mucklow turned to go.

"One more thing," Cooper said. "Tell the captain to stay below 10,000 feet [3,048 m]. Tell him to keep the flaps down and to cruise at 200 mph [322 kph]. No faster!"

"Yes sir," Tina said. Once again, she started to go.

"Wait," said Cooper. "I'm coming with you."

At the cockpit door, Cooper pushed Tina inside.

"She has my orders, Captain," he said. "If you don't follow them to the letter, I'll blow up the plane. Any questions?"

The crew was silent. Cooper looked at them, one by one.

"There's one more thing," he said. "I'm going to close the cockpit door now. And I want it to stay closed. If it opens, the whole plane goes."

With that, D. B. Cooper slammed the door and walked away.

Captain Scott set a course for Reno. He kept the plane below 10,000 feet (3,048 m). He flew no faster than 200 mph (322 kph). And he kept the cockpit door closed. He was going to obey Cooper's orders, no matter what.

At 7:50 P.M., a light flashed on the panel board. It meant that the rear door was being opened.

"Captain," Tina Mucklow said, "don't you think we should . . ."

"Nothing," Scott said quickly. "We should do nothing but continue to Reno. Those are our orders. And that's what we're going to do."

At 8:10 P.M., another light flashed. It meant that the rear boarding ramp was being lowered.

The captain still would not open the door. But he did turn on the loudspeaker system.

"Is everything all right out there?" he asked.

There was no answer.

"Do you think he jumped, sir?" Tina asked.

"Yes," the captain said, "I do. But we're still not going to open the door. We're not going to open it until we get to Reno."

Tina was silent for a moment. Then she said, "He must be crazy, he must be mad, if he jumped."

Captain Scott felt the same way. The plane was passing over the Cascade Mountains in south-

[15]

*The latest clue in the D. B. Cooper case
was uncovered in 1980 along the banks of the
Columbia River in Washington. The serial
numbers of the bills matched those given
to the hijacker in 1971.*

ern Washington. Wild and covered with forests, they are hardly a good place to land in a parachute. To make things even worse, a snowstorm was raging. It was impossible to see!

How could anyone jump into that storm, into those mountains, and live?

Captain Scott shook his head. But he kept the door closed. And he kept the plane on course.

Two hours later, the 727 landed in Reno. Only then did the captain leave his seat. Slowly, he opened the cockpit door. The cabin was empty.

Police officers in four states were sent out to search for signs of Cooper. A unit from the Army's Fort Lewis combed the Cascade Mountains. So did the Third Army Cavalry.

And while hundreds of people searched on the ground, two Army helicopters flew back and forth along the route the plane had taken. But no one found anything.

In the spring, when the snows had melted, search parties combed the mountains again. But they did not find a single trace of Cooper, the parachutes, or the money.

Then, in February of 1980, an eight-year-old

boy was playing along the banks of the Columbia River in Washington State. He tripped over some packages lying in the sand. When he opened the packages, he discovered piles of wet and decomposed $20 bills.

Detectives checked the serial numbers. Sure enough, they were the same bills Cooper had been given as ransom. But this only accounted for a few thousand dollars. What happened to the rest of the money? And what ever happened to D. B. Cooper?

VERA'S DIAMOND

The diamond was as big as a walnut. It was worth $300,000. And Vera Krupp wore it everywhere.

Vera lived alone on a ranch near Las Vegas, Nevada. Everyone knew her. Brown-haired and lovely, she rode around town in a shiny new Lincoln. She was very friendly. And very rich.

Vera liked Las Vegas. She liked the people and the bright lights. She liked the nightclubs and the gambling. But she could never live in town, she said. For her, the ranch was home. She always felt safe there. It was the most peaceful place on earth.

What happened on the night of April 10, 1959, however, changed all that forever.

April 10 was a Friday. And at the Krupp ranch, Fridays were quiet. Vera usually spent them with the foreman of her ranch, Harold Brotherson. They looked over the record books and discussed ranch business. Except for them, the big house was empty. It was the help's night off.

The evening of April 10 began like any other Friday evening. Vera and Brotherson were in the living room drinking coffee. The ranch record books were on the table.

At eight o'clock, there was a knock at the front door.

"I'll see who it is," Vera said, getting up. "I'm not expecting anyone." Then she hurried down the hall.

"Who is it?" Vera called out when she got to the front door.

"My name is John Peterson," a man answered. "I've come to talk about your driveway."

Vera had been looking for someone to repair her road and driveway. So, smiling, she opened the door to let the man in.

"Good evening, Mrs. Krupp," he said.

Then he pulled a gun out of his pocket and pointed it straight at her. Vera stepped back. She could hardly believe what was happening. At the same instant, two other men came inside. They had guns too.

"Don't worry, Vera," the first man said. "Just do what you're told and no one will get hurt."

Vera was so shocked that she couldn't speak.

One of the men pushed her aside and walked down the hallway. He went to the living room. There he found Brotherson, quietly drinking his coffee.

"What the—" Brotherson said to the gunman. He pushed his chair back and started to get up.

"Take it easy, mister," the gunman said. "Don't get any big ideas. Just put your hands behind your back and stand still."

Brotherson did as he was told. The gunman slipped handcuffs on him. Then he ordered him to walk down the hall.

Vera was silent when Brotherson got to

her. She seemed to be all right, except for one thing. Her ring finger was scraped and bleeding. And her wonderful diamond ring was gone.

"OK, you two," the gunman said. "On the floor! Hurry up! We don't have all night!"

The crooks tied Vera and Brotherson together, back to back, with wire. Then they sealed their eyes shut with heavy tape. But even that was not enough.

They took a poker and a tong from the fireplace and tied them together in the form of an X. Then they tied one end of the huge X to Vera and Brotherson. They tied the other end to a heavy chair. Finally they wrapped everything —Vera, Brotherson, and the chair—in a giant rug.

When they were finished, the crooks searched the house for other things to steal. They took a camera and some cash. But they already had the big prize, the diamond. In less than half an hour, they were gone.

"It's up to you, Vera," Brotherson said when he heard the front door closing. "I'll never get out of these handcuffs."

"I know, Hal," Vera said. "I'm trying."

She twisted and turned her hands over and over. But the wires which tied them were strong and tight.

"I can't do it, Hal," she said. "I just can't."

But even as she said it, Vera felt one of the knots come loose.

Quickly, she slipped out one hand, then the other. Then she began to untie the rest of the knots. Soon she and Brotherson were free. They raced to the telephone.

Vera picked up the receiver.

"It's dead, Hal," she said. "They must have cut the wires."

They ran to Vera's car, parked in the driveway. But the keys were missing, taken by the crooks.

They ran to the van which Brotherson used for ranch business. The gas tank had been emptied.

"Come on," Vera said, "to the bunkhouse."

The bunkhouse was where the ranch hands lived. It was about one-quarter mile (.4 km) away from the main house. Vera knew that most of the men went to town on Friday nights. But someone, she hoped, would be there to help them.

Quickly, Vera and Hal made their way across the dark grounds. Soon they could see lights shining through the trees. Then they saw the house itself. A man was sitting by the window.

"Thank God!" Vera said to Hal. "Someone is there."

The man Vera saw was Tom Richards.

Richards called to the two other men who were playing cards in the kitchen. Together, they ran outside.

"We've been robbed!" Brotherson called out. Then he turned around so the men could see his handcuffs. "Get the hacksaw, Tom!" he said. "See if you can get these off me!"

While Tom worked on the handcuffs, the other men carried cans of gasoline to the car. By the time the handcuffs were off, Vera was behind the wheel, ready to go.

By 11:30 P.M., the Clark County Sheriff's Office had the whole story. The next day, it made headlines all over the United States.

The FBI entered the Krupp Diamond Case almost

at once. Descriptions of the crime and the diamond were sent to offices across the United States. All agents were asked to be on the alert.

In Las Vegas itself, agents searched Vera's house for clues. When they didn't find any, they turned to a study of their own records. They looked up other jewel robberies that had taken place in Nevada and the states near Nevada. They hoped that one of them would provide a lead.

After days of study, agents came up with the name of a possible suspect: John William Hagenson. Hagenson was wanted for an April 1 jewel robbery. It had taken place in Los Angeles. But it had been done in just the same way as the Krupp robbery. What was more, agents learned, Hagenson had been in Las Vegas on April 10. And he had been seen leaving town late that night with some friends.

Hagenson was already being hunted for the April 1 job. Now, more agents joined in.

Three days later, Las Vegas agents turned up the name of another suspect. He was Marion Carter Bowman. He lived in Las Vegas. And he had been broke, his friends said, until April 10. After that, he had had "a lot" of money. And after that, he had left town.

The FBI looked up Bowman's record. He was thirty-eight years old, they learned, and a golf pro. He had also spent time in jail for armed robbery. Bowman's name and picture were added to Hagenson's. Both were sent to FBI offices around the country.

Within two days, agents in Los Angeles, New York, and Miami Beach, and smaller cities in between, had hit the streets. They spoke to everyone they could find who had ever known Hagenson or Bowman. They couldn't find any trace of Bowman. But within a week, they had picked up Hagenson's trail. He had been seen in Miami right after the robbery. A few days later, he had been seen in Palm Springs, and after that, in New York. The last person to see him had seen him in Chicago. Agents were sure that it would not be long before they caught up with him.

Three days later, on April 21, word came in from agents in Bossier City, Louisiana. A motel owner there had called the police because "some

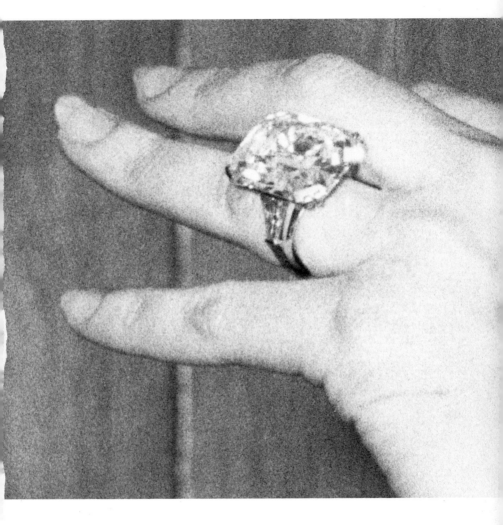

*The 33.19-carat Krupp diamond
is said to be one of the most
perfect stones in the world.*

people" at his motel were "acting strange." The police came and found Hagenson, Bowman, and a third man, named John Sneed Davie.

The men were taken to FBI headquarters and questioned. They said that they didn't know anything about a robbery in Las Vegas. And they had "never heard" of Vera Krupp or her diamond.

The agents were sure that the men were lying. But unless they found the diamond, they couldn't prove it. They searched the motel room, the grounds, and the cars the men had driven. But the diamond was not there.

The agents had no choice. They turned Hagenson over to the Los Angeles police for the April 1 robbery, and they let Bowman and Davie go.

During all this time, the FBI kept in touch with Vera. They told her how the case was going. They told her when new information or new suspects turned up. But, even now, they could not tell her anything about the diamond itself. They had no idea where it was.

"Do you think you'll ever find it?" Vera asked each time she spoke to an agent. "Do you think I'll ever get it back?"

"We're working on it, Vera," was all they could say. "We're doing our best."

FBI agents continued to search for the diamond in and around Bossier City. But it didn't turn up. A few days later, they learned why: the diamond was in Newark, New Jersey. How had it gotten there? The FBI in Newark had no idea. But one of the agents on the case had spent days talking to jewelers and ex-crooks. For a while, he had gotten nowhere. And then it happened. One jeweler told him that a "new rock" was making the rounds. It was, the man said, "a very large piece of ice." And it had been "lifted," so he had heard, "off some woman in Nevada." The man who was trying to sell it was named Julius ("Jully") Berger.

The agent put Berger's name through the FBI computer. He was an old-timer in Newark, it seemed. He had been a fence for years. But he had never taken part in a robbery. Chances were that he had not been in on the Krupp robbery either. But he could lead them to the diamond. The search for Berger was on.

Two days passed without a clue. Then, on

May 21, Berger's car was found. It was parked on a side street in Jersey City. Agents were posted to watch it around the clock.

Nothing happened on the first night—or the second. But at 5:30 in the morning of the third day, a man came walking, almost running, down the empty street. When he got to the car, he stopped. He reached into his pocket and took out a set of keys. Then he opened the front door.

The agents surrounded him. They had found Julius Berger.

Berger was not upset or even surprised.

"FBI, right?" he said to the agents. "OK, I'm cool. I know why you're here. I had the ring, but I don't have it now. I've been trying to sell it for another guy. I gave it back to him yesterday."

"In that case, Jully," an agent said, "you won't have any trouble telling us where he is, will you?"

For a moment, Berger did not say anything.

"C'mon, Jully," the agent said, "unless you want to get booked for robbery!"

"OK, OK," Berger said. "The guy you want

is Jimmy Reves. He's at the Cadillac Motel in Elizabeth. He's there with his wife. I swear it."

That was all the agents needed to hear. They raced to the Cadillac Motel.

"This is the FBI," they called out as they knocked on the door of Room 24. "We have a warrant for your arrest, Reves. Open up."

No one answered. The agents called out one more time.

"Open up! We're coming in one way or the other!"

Still no answer. The agents forced open the door. They found Reves and his wife huddled in the bathroom.

"We don't know anything," Reves said. "You've got no right to bust in like this."

One agent put handcuffs on Reves. The others searched the room. In a jacket that was hanging in the closet, they found the diamond from Vera Krupp's ring.

Now Reves was ready to talk. John Hagenson, he said, was the "brains" behind the job. It had been his idea from the start. He had asked

Bowman to find "three or four other men" who could pull it off with him. Bowman had found Davie. And Davie had gotten in touch with Reves.

Reves admitted that he had carried the diamond out of the state. He had taped it to the inside of his pants. Then, with his wife, he had gone to Bossier City and the Empire Motel. The whole gang, which had split up after the robbery, had agreed to meet there by the weekend.

Within two days, Hagenson had arrived. Then John Davie and his wife showed up, and then Marion Carter Bowman.

Reves had wanted to throw a big party. But Hagenson had told him to calm down.

"It's not over yet," Hagenson had said. "We've got to get rid of the ring first. After we sell it—that's when we'll have a party."

For several days, the whole gang traveled together. First they went to Miami Beach. But they could not sell the ring there. They tried St. Louis, Missouri; Cairo, Illinois; and Cape Girardeau, Missouri. But no one would buy the diamond. It was "too hot."

The gang returned to Bossier City to plan

their next move. Chicago, they thought, would be their best bet. In Chicago there would be lots of fences and lots of buyers.

"Can you handle it alone?" Hagenson had asked Reves. "Then the rest of us can lay low right here. No one will be looking for us in Bossier City."

"I'll handle it," Reves said. "No problem."

Early in the morning of May 15, Reves set out. That night, the police, called in by the motel owner, arrived. They picked up Hagenson, Bowman, and Davie. Though they did not know it at the time, they had missed Reves—and the diamond—by less than a day.

Reves got to Chicago. But he could not sell the ring there. One of his contacts told him to try Newark. There was a man there, he said, named Jully Berger. He would be able to sell it if anybody could.

Reves hid the diamond in the case of his electric shaver. Then he and his wife took off for Newark. They found Jully all right, and showed him the diamond. He said he could sell it for them easily.

The rest is history. On May 23, at 5:30 A.M., Jully Berger was picked up by the FBI. At 6:30 A.M. Reves was arrested. By noon the next day, Bowman and Davie were taken in.

It was all over. The Case of Vera's Diamond was closed. The search had taken hundreds of agents to dozens of cities across the United States. But in the end, FBI agents got their men. And Vera got her diamond.

THE GREAT
TRAIN ROBBERY

One member of the gang cut the phone wires.

A second man blacked out the green GO signal.

A third turned on the red STOP signal.

Then they joined the rest of the gang in the bushes beside the rail track. It was 2:00 A.M. The train was due any minute.

They heard it, and then they saw it. A 2,000 horsepower, diesel engine, twelve-car mail train. The Royal Mail train. It was racing down the tracks at 70 mph (113 kmp), bound for London. It was carrying £1,785,714 ($5,000,000), at least, in cash and bank notes.

The engineer on the train that night was Jack Mills. He was glad the long trip from Glasgow was almost over. They had pulled out at 7:00 P.M., and had covered almost 400 miles (644 km). Now London was less than an hour away. He would have a nice, cool glass of ale at the station, Jack thought. Then he would go home.

Jack wasn't even thinking about how much money the train was carrying. After all, no one had robbed a Royal Mail train in one hundred and twenty-five years. No one had even tried. It just wasn't done.

The train was coming out of a curve when Jack saw the red signal light. He brought the train to a stop, and waited.

"What's up, Jack?" David Whitby, the fireman, asked.

"Nothing much, I'm sure," Jack said. "Maybe some repair up ahead."

Then he stood up and opened the door. He looked out along the tracks. But he didn't see anything.

"Why don't you hop down, David?" the engineer said. "There should be a phone back along the track. Call the signal station and see if you can find out what's happening."

"Right Jack," David said. He climbed down from the car and walked quickly away.

The engineer settled back to wait. The night was very dark and still. For a moment, he thought he heard footsteps outside. But then the sound stopped.

"I must be hearing things," he thought to himself. Then he sat back once again.

All at once, Jack saw a man on the steps of the cab. He was wearing a mask and carrying a club.

"I didn't think," Jack said later. "I just threw myself at him and we went at it. Then someone else grabbed me from behind. I couldn't fight them both."

The second man held Jack, while the first man hit him with the club. Jack fell to the ground.

"Don't look up or you'll get some more," he heard someone say.

With that, Jack Mills lay still.

At that very moment, David Whitby reached the telephone post. He opened the box and tried to call the station.

The phone was dead. The wires, he saw, had been cut. Who would do that? David asked himself. And why?

The next thing he knew, he was on the ground. Someone had pushed him into the gully beside the tracks. When he looked up, a man with a club was standing over him.

"All right! All right, mate!" David said. "I'm on your side!"

The man pulled David to his feet and marched him back to the cab. He was thrown to the floor beside Jack Mills.

With the engineer and the fireman out of the way, the gang went to work. In silence, they unhooked the first two cars from the rest of the train. The first two cars were the "high value" cars, the cars which held the money. The other cars held only regular mail.

The men worked quietly and quickly. The postal workers in the cars had no idea that anything special was going on. They were used to the train stopping and starting as signal lights changed. To them, this was just one more stop along the way.

Soon the front cars were free. The gang returned to the cab.

"Let's go, mate," one of them said to Mills. "Get this thing moving. And stop when I say stop, or you'll get more of this!"

He shook his club above Jack's head.

Slowly, Jack pulled the train out. He was bleeding and he was dizzy, but he did as he was told.

The train was stopped about 2 miles (3 km) up the track. Jack and David were taken out of the cab. They were handcuffed together and made to lie down beside the tracks. One of the robbers was left to guard them.

The postal workers in the front two cars still didn't know what was happening. They had locked the doors from the inside, as they always did, when they started the trip. They would unlock them when they reached London. In the meantime, they were going about their work, as usual.

"Suddenly," one worker said later, "there was a great crashing sound. Glass came flying through the air. We were all stunned. I, for one, couldn't even move. I thought the train had been bombed. I thought it was blowing up."

But it wasn't a bomb, the worker soon saw. It was a masked man smashing the windows with an ax. In the next moment, the car was filled with masked men. They shook clubs and axes at the terrified workers.

"On the floor, all of you," the head man said. "And stay there! God help you if you move!"

The workers huddled on the floor. One man stood over them. The rest formed themselves into a line, a human chain. It went from the inside of the train to a van that was parked beside the tracks. Sack after sack of money was passed down the line and loaded onto the truck. Jack Mills and David Whitby watched the whole thing. So did the man who was guarding them. He smiled broadly as the money moved along.

"Here mate," he said to David. "You can have a puff of this cigarette, if you like. Maybe I'll get your address," he added, "and send you a few quid later."

Soon it was all over. The "human chain" broke up and became a group of men. They climbed onto the truck. Then they were gone.

The next day, the robbery was the talk of all England. It was almost too big to be believed. The gang had made off with over £2,500,000 ($7,000,000)!

Many people cheered the robbers. To some, they were heroes. After all, they had stolen more money than had ever been stolen before. And they hadn't killed anyone to do it!

When the news broke in America, *The New York Times* said the crooks had been "daring and bold and intelligent." One magazine article even said that they had "put American robbers to shame!"

During all this time, the British police were silent. Newspaper reporters questioned them. But they had "no comment." With a crime so huge, it was hard to know where to begin.

Scotland Yard sent detectives. They searched the coaches, inside and out. They searched the tracks for miles in both directions. They drove up and down the roads looking for something—anything—that might give them a lead.

Teams of detectives went to every house, farmhouse, school, hospital, and store in the area. They spoke to everyone, from farmers working in the fields to children walking on the roads. And wherever they went, they asked people to call them if they saw or thought of anything at all that might help.

Hundreds of people called the police with "tips." Every tip, no matter how small or silly it seemed, was followed up. One of them, from a

British detectives
sift through gravel
and soil next to
the train tracks for
clues after the
Great Train Robbery.

farmer named John Maris, became the first big break.

Maris said he thought the police should check a local farmhouse called "Leatherslade." It was a fine house, Maris said. It was tucked way back on the Leatherslade property, far from the public road. But he was sure that "something wrong" was going on there.

New owners had moved in about a month before the robbery. They never came to town. They didn't work the fields. That was strange enough. But that wasn't all. One day, as Maris was taking a shortcut across the property, he saw something even stranger. All the windows on the farmhouse had been blacked out.

Maris stayed away after that.

"Whoever was living there," he said, "it was clear that they wanted to be left alone."

But after the robbery, he thought about Leatherslade more and more. Finally, he drove over, "just to have a look." He saw a van covered with a giant tarp, hidden in the orchard. Another van was in the yard. And in the fields behind the house were two jeeps.

Maris called the police. They came at once. In a ditch behind the house, they found a pile of empty mail bags. In the house itself were more. And in one of the rooms, there were strips of paper marked "National Provincial Bank."

There was no doubt about it. Leatherslade had been the robbers' hide-out. From the looks of it, the robbers themselves had been there that morning. They had left in a great hurry. Dishes half-filled with food were on the kitchen table. Sleeping bags and blankets were on the floor.

A crew of detectives from Scotland Yard came to Leatherslade the next day. They divided the house into sections. They searched each section, inch by inch. And the careful work paid off. Fifteen sets of fingerprints were found!

Now the police had something to tell the reporters. The gang had had a wonderful plan for the robbery itself, they said. Everything had been worked out carefully. But after the robbery, the gang had been sloppy. Very sloppy. They should have gone as far from the scene of the crime as possible. They should have gone as quickly as possible. Instead they had hidden in a farmhouse

only a few miles away. They had run off in a panic, leaving fingerprints behind them!

The police were delighted. The robbery that had been "too big to be believed" might now turn out to be a big flop!

The things that happened in the next two weeks gave them even more reason for cheering. First, a young couple hiking in a forest near the farmhouse found a suitcase. It was stuffed with money.

The couple called the police. When the police searched the area, they found yet another suitcase. It, too, was full of money.

They took both cases to the police station. It took the officers six hours to count all the money. How much was there? £107,143 ($300,000)!

The next week, 8 miles (13 km) down the

An aerial view of
Leatherslade Farm,
hideout of the gang
that held up the
Royal Mail Train.

road, police found a van that had been left in a parking lot. They searched it on the spot, but found nothing. Then, just to be on the safe side, they took it to police headquarters. There they stripped it. It was papered with money—£30,000 ($84,000) to be exact—packed between the metal outside walls and the inner lining.

Four days later, police found a laundry sack with £50,000 ($140,000) in it. The sack had been left in a phone booth.

The crooks were on the run all right. And they were actually dumping money as they went.

Soon the arrests began. First were two gang members who had tried to rent garage space from a Mrs. Ethel Clark of Bournemouth.

"They were nervous the whole while," Mrs. Clark said. "And they kept looking around them with worried eyes."

Still, she might not have done anything. But then one of them pulled out a wad of money as big "as a telephone book." Mrs. Clark slipped into her house and called the police.

Two officers came over. They tried to question the men. And the men tried to run away. They were arrested and taken to police headquarters. Their van was searched. Bundles and bundles of bank notes were found, almost £142,857 ($400,000) worth.

Over the next few weeks, ten more arrests were made. Some of them were made quickly and easily. They were the ones which did not involve a great deal of money. And the people were charged with "receiving stolen goods" rather than with the robbery itself.

The big arrests, though, were anything but easy. James Daly, for example, whose fingerprints had been found at Leatherslade, almost got away.

The police had received a "tip" on where Daly was, a two-story house on a quiet London street. When they got there, the front door was locked. No one answered their call to "open up."

The officers spread out. Five of them climbed to the second-story balcony. They broke a window and went inside. They were just in time to see Daly climbing out another window and onto the roof.

They chased him, and had almost caught him, when he jumped over the side. Unluckily for him, he landed right in the middle of the officers waiting below.

Several other top gang members were caught in the weeks to come. The police were sure that soon they would find the "brain" behind the robbery, the man who had planned it. But so far, they didn't even know his name. They called him by the code name the robbers used: Johnny Rainbow. Newspapers added a nickname: "The Major."

There were many theories about who and what Johnny Rainbow was. Some people said he had been a hero during the war. And that he had "gone to the bad" when he was thrown out of the army for gambling.

Maybe even the robbers didn't know who Johnny Rainbow really was. In any case, they weren't telling. Still, with so many arrests already made, and more being made almost weekly, the hardest part of the search seemed to be over. The leader would soon be found. And so would the almost £1,785,714 ($5,000,000) that was still missing. At least, that's what the police thought.

Soon the trial began for the people who had already been arrested. Twelve men were found guilty of robbery and sentenced to prison. The police had worked hard and well. But still, when the trial was over, there was a restless feeling in the air, for the case itself was not over. The leader of the gang was still missing. And so was most of the money.

It is now almost twenty years since the Great Train Robbery. Johnny Rainbow has never been found. Neither has the money.

Does Johnny have the money with him? Or is it hidden in the fields and on the hillsides near Leatherslade? Will it ever be found? Will Johnny Rainbow ever come forward and tell us the whole story?

All we can do is wonder.

THE SWINDLE
OF THE CENTURY

Cassie Bigley Chadwick was born on a farm. Her family was very poor. They all worked very hard.

Cassie hated being poor. And she hated hard work. She did everything she could to get out of it. Mostly, she lied.

She made believe she was too sick to work. She made believe she was too weak. Once, she made believe she was blind.

By the time she was fifteen, Cassie had turned lying into an art. Not even her mother knew when to believe her. By the time she was twenty-five, she had turned it into a business.

For a while, it brought her over $1,000,000 a year.

Cassie Bigley had left the farm by the time she began her "business." She was married to a doctor, Leroy Chadwick, and lived in Cleveland.

Chadwick had plenty of money, more than Cassie had ever had before. But her plans were even bigger. Getting a rich husband had been the first step. Now she planned and plotted and waited to begin the second.

It happened at a dinner party Cassie gave. Many of Dr. Chadwick's friends were there. One of them was a lawyer. His clients were the rich businessmen of Cleveland.

Cassie could see that the lawyer was very nosy. He loved gossip. He loved to hear it. And he loved to spread it. That made him just right for the plan Cassie had in mind.

During the evening, Cassie kept her eyes on him. She heard him say that he was going to New York on business at the end of the week. She also heard him name the hotel where he would be staying.

The next day, Cassie made her own plans to visit New York. Once there, she checked into the Holland House. It was one of the fanciest hotels around. Then she went shopping for dresses and furs.

The next morning, Cassie dressed in her loveliest gown. A hairdresser came to fix her hair. When she was sure she looked "picture perfect," Cassie set out. She went to the lobby of the hotel where the lawyer was staying. She sat down on the couch in the middle of the lobby. She wanted to be sure that everyone could see her.

Soon the lawyer came into the lobby, just as Cassie had hoped he would. She saw him right away. But she made believe that she did not. Instead, she stood up. She waited for him to see her. Soon he came across the lobby, calling her name.

"Mrs. Chadwick!" he cried out. "How nice to see you! I had no idea you were in New York!"

"Why, Mr. Williams," Cassie said smiling. "What a pleasant surprise!"

They chatted for a few minutes. Then, with a friendly smile, Cassie said that she had to go.

"But if you are not busy tomorrow," she said, "perhaps you will join me for lunch. I am having a small party in my rooms at the Holland House."

The lawyer said that he would be there. Cassie wrapped her furs around her and left.

The next morning, Cassie awoke early. She had coffee alone in her room. Then she slowly walked to the telephone. She made one call. When she hung up, she was smiling. Everything was working out just as she had planned.

At 12:00 noon, her guests arrived. As always, Cassie was a good hostess. But when the others left, she asked the lawyer to stay behind. Then she popped her big question.

"Do you know Andrew Carnegie?" she asked.

At the mention of the famous millionaire's name, the lawyer stood up.

"Why no," he said, "I don't."

"Would you like to meet him?" Cassie asked.

"It would be a great pleasure," he said.

"Well," said Cassie, "I am going to visit him at three o'clock this afternoon. If you like, you may come along."

"Thank you," the lawyer answered. "I would like that. Thank you very much indeed!"

That afternoon, Cassie and Mr. Williams took a carriage up Fifth Avenue. They rode past the mansions of America's richest people. Soon they reached Central Park. The Carnegie mansion, between 90th and 91st Streets, was almost in view.

"You won't mind, will you," Cassie said, "if I go in first? Mr. Carnegie doesn't see strangers. I will have to tell him about you before I bring you in."

"Of course, Mrs. Chadwick," the lawyer said. "I don't mind at all."

The carriage stopped. Mr. Williams helped Cassie out. She walked to the front of the mansion and knocked on the door.

A maid opened it. Cassie stepped quickly inside. The door closed behind her.

"Yes?" the maid said. "May I help you?"

"I'm here to see the housekeeper," Cassie said smiling. "I spoke to her on the telephone this morning. She knows I am coming."

The girl left. Soon the housekeeper came down.

"Good afternoon," Cassie said. "Thank you for seeing me. I won't take up much of your time."

The two women went into the housekeeper's room.

"I would like to ask you," Cassie said, "about a girl who wishes to be my maid. She said she once worked here, and that you would put in a good word for her. Her name is Freda Swensen."

The housekeeper looked puzzled.

"No one by that name has ever worked here," she said.

"What!" Cassie said. "But that's awful! The girl must have made up the whole story. She didn't think I would check. Some people are such terrible liars!"

The housekeeper agreed. Cassie stood up to go.

"Oh, before I go," she said, "may I use your table to write some notes? If I may, I can drop them off on my way downtown. It would save me ever so much time!"

"Of course," the housekeeper said.

Cassie sat down. She worked for ten minutes.

Then, holding the papers in one hand, she left. When she got to the carriage, she smiled sadly at Mr. Williams.

"I'm so sorry," she said. "Mr. Carnegie was not feeling very well. He couldn't see anyone but me. But he said you might come and see him some other time. I hope you understand."

"My dear, of course I do," the lawyer said. He began to help Cassie into the carriage.

At that moment, Cassie dropped the notes she had just written. The lawyer bent down to pick them up for her. Cassie knew that he would try to steal a look at them. She gave him plenty of time.

The four papers were "promissory notes." Each one "promised to pay" Cassie Chadwick $500,000! That amounted, in all, to half a million dollars! They were "signed" (by Cassie, of course) with Andrew Carnegie's name.

The lawyer gulped and handed the papers back to Cassie. He was pretending that he had not read them.

"Thank you so much," Cassie said. Then she sat back in the cab and sighed.

"Is anything the matter, my dear?" the lawyer said.

For a moment, Cassie was silent. She picked up the papers and looked at them. Than she put them down.

"I must confess," she said, "that I have kept something from you."

The lawyer tried to look calm.

"You don't have to tell me anything," he said.

"But I want to," Cassie said. "That is the real reason I asked you to come with me today. I must talk to someone. I need advice."

"Oh, my dear," the lawyer said, "you may trust me. Whatever you tell me will be our secret."

"This is so very difficult," Cassie said. "I've never told anyone at all. But now I suppose that I must. You see, Mr. Carnegie wishes to leave me a certain sum of money. But he doesn't want anyone to know about it."

"Oh?" the lawyer said.

"You're probably wondering," Cassie went on, "why Mr. Carnegie would want to leave me anything at all."

"No, no, my dear," said the lawyer. "That is none of my business."

But Cassie knew that that was exactly what he had been thinking about. In fact, this was the most important part of her plan.

"I will tell you anyway," she said slowly. "Then you will understand why all this is so secret."

The lawyer looked at her. He waited for her to go on.

"Mr. Carnegie," said Cassie, lowering her eyes, "is my father." She looked at the lawyer to see how he had taken the news. He was quiet. Cassie knew that he was waiting for her to tell him more.

"Mr. Carnegie never married my mother. But he loved her all the same, that I know," she said. "And she loved him. He stopped seeing her when I was born, but he always sent her money. And he always cared about me."

As she said this, Cassie began to cry. Mr. Williams gave her his handkerchief.

"I'm so sorry," she said. "Please forgive me. It's just that I've never told anyone about this."

She wiped her eyes. Then she went on.

"My mother died when I was three years old. I was raised by foster parents in Canada. But through all these years, Mr. Carnegie has taken care of me. Now that he is old, he wishes to give me money in trust. It will be mine when he dies. But of course, it must be a secret."

At this, Cassie sighed deeply. "Mr. Carnegie said I would need a good lawyer," she went on. "Someone who can draw up the papers. I can't go to my husband's lawyer, for all this is a secret even from my husband. But I thought," she said, "that you might do it for me."

"Of course," Mr. Williams said, "of course."

Then Cassie told him exactly how much

Mrs. Cassie Chadwick in finery acquired through one of the most clever—and successful—swindles of the century.

money Mr. Carnegie wished to leave her: *$11,000,000 in stocks and bonds!*

The next day, the lawyer brought Cassie the paper he had written up. It stated that "Mr. Andrew J. Carnegie" was "holding" for "Mrs. Cassie L. Chadwick of Cleveland" $11,000,000 in stocks and bonds. "These monies," he had written, "shall be turned over to Mrs. Chadwick upon Mr. Carnegie's death."

"I thank you from the bottom of my heart," Cassie said. "Who else could I have trusted with my secret?"

When the lawyer was gone, Cassie sat down and laughed. It would take him about two weeks, she thought, to spread her "secret" all over Cleveland. But just to be on the safe side, she gave him three.

October turned to November. Then, Cassie thought, the time was right. She went from businessman to businessman. She went from bank to bank. Everyone was willing to lend money to her. No one asked her to prove that she would be able to repay it. They all knew her "secret." They "knew" she would receive $11,000,000 when old Andrew Carnegie died.

One man, Charles T. Beckwith, was especially eager to loan money to Cassie. He found out that he could charge her higher rates of interest than he could charge anyone else. (Cassie didn't care what the rate of interest was. She was never going to repay the loan anyway.) Within a few weeks of their meeting, Beckwith had loaned Cassie all of his own money: $100,000. A few weeks after that, he began to lend her money which belonged to his bank, the Citizen's National Bank of Oberlin. Within a year, Cassie had borrowed $250,000 from the bank. That was half of all the money people had deposited there.

Over the next several years, Cassie became a legend in Cleveland. She bought cars by the dozens. She bought priceless oil paintings, diamonds, rubies, and pearls and gave them away to friends. She bought furs, dresses, hats, shoes, furniture. She bought twenty-seven pianos and gave them away as gifts. She hired an entire train to take a party to New York for the opera. She was known in the best circles as "the fabulous Mrs. Chadwick."

Cassie paid for the things she bought. She paid for them with the money she borrowed. But she did not repay the loans. She couldn't. They were too large. Sooner or later, things had to catch up with her. In October 1907, they did.

A banker named Herbert D. Newton wanted to collect the $190,000 he had loaned her. Cassie asked him to wait. He began a lawsuit to collect the money.

The people at the Citizen's National Bank of Oberlin heard about it. They worried. If Mrs. Chadwick would not pay her debt to Newton, perhaps she would not pay her debt to the bank either. Word spread. The people who had put their money in the bank rushed to take it out. Soon the bank ran out of money to give them. It closed its doors.

Newspaper headlines from the Cassie Chadwick case.

MRS. CHADWICK TALKS; NOW IN TOMBS CELL

Doesn't Deny She Is Mme. De Vere—Promises Explanation.

VAIN HUNT FOR BONDSMA[N]

Prosecutor Says More Charges Follow—Ohio Jury Votes to Indict Woman.

When eight hours of frant[ic] effort failed to reveal a bondsman to put up $30,000 for Mrs. Cass[ie] Chadwick, she was locked up in the back ... o'clock last night. She ... rooms, before ... ed States parlor, board

$60,000 CHADWICK GEMS FOUND BY DETECTIVES

Woman Placed Them in a Bank for Safekeeping.

TWO JEWELS IN WASHINGTON

Diamond Sunburst and Emerald Ring Now In ... ry Vault—In- ...inues.

VOL. LIV....NO. 17,219.

MRS. CHADWICK GUILTY IS VERDICT OF JURY

Got Checks on National Banks Certified Without Funds.

BREAKS DOWN AT THE NEWS

Maximum Penalty is $10,000 Fine and Two Years in Prison on Each of Seven Counts.

CLEVELAND, Ohio, March 11.—Mrs. Cassie L. Chadwick was found guilty to-night of conspiring to defraud in procuring the certification of checks on a National bank when there were no funds in the bank to her credit. She was found guilty on every count of the indictment upon which the jury was at liberty to judge her—seven in all.

The original indictment contained sixteen counts. Two of these were ruled out during the trial by Judge Taylor, and of the remaining fourteen one-half charged her with securing the certification of checks without having the proper entries ...

of Unite[d] ... *Times.*
placed up—The secret
An atta[ck] n investi-
lasted fully l[ ] Chad-
cries being [ ] jewels
outside. Th e care
attendance [ ]
gently. In a strict
time she enter than
Chadwick wa[s] ew-
composure, an[d]]-
jail. From the
shal's office [ ] on
closed behind
ous moaning cers

The verd line,
torneys ir ffect
the Distr'
lant ove
after th
"I dor
Not n
the p[ ]
It has
believe
given."
Judge
had ho[pe]
is not
the hig
finish."
After
continued
sation,
few minu
was sent
and wher
"She is
might be
gone thro
commence
gether too
not appre
ever."
Dr. Ch

Word spread further. Other businessmen asked to be repaid. Banks asked. They all got the same answer: "Later."

How did Cassie handle the storm? She took a train to New York. There, on a cold snowy morning in December, she was arrested. She spent a week in New York's Tombs Prison. Then she was sent back to Cleveland to stand trial. She was sentenced to ten years in the Ohio State Prison. For a while, police and detectives searched for the money they thought she had hidden away. After all, she had "borrowed" millions and millions of dollars! She must have put some of it somewhere.

But while they found some of her jewels, they never did find any money. "The fabulous Mrs. Chadwick" had spent it all.

Cassie died two years after she was let out of prison. She was buried quietly, the shame of her family.

To some people, Cassie had been a "common criminal." To others, she was a "super swindler," a "fabulous fake."

We don't really know how she felt about what she did. But perhaps, in the end, she was pleased. After all, she had lived out her dream. It hadn't lasted. But for a time, the poor farm girl had had everything she had ever wanted. For a little while, she had had it all.

THE INCREDIBLE
BRINKS JOB

It is early Tuesday evening, January 17, 1950. The city of Boston is quiet and cold.

Prince Street, in the North End of Boston, is empty. Lights shine in the houses on the right side of the street. They shine in the windows of the Northside Terminal Building on the other side of the street. But no one is on the streets now. It is too cold.

The Terminal Building is a brick building, two stories high. The first floor is a garage. The second floor has offices. The garage and the offices belong to a famous delivery company: Brinks, Inc. It is famous because it delivers money.

At 6:00 P.M., the first van pulls into the garage. It looks more like a tank than a van. Its sides are bulletproof. So is the glass in the window of the cab. Bars cover the small windows in the huge back doors.

The driver stops the van. He jumps down and walks quickly to the back. He looks around carefully as he goes. Then he taps on the back doors. The guards inside open them and jump down.

The men unload the huge bags of money from the van. They carry them to the office on the second floor. There, other workers count the money. They sign the report forms. Then they put the money into the safe.

Soon, other vans pull into the garage. They too are unloaded quickly. All the money is put into the safe.

By 6:50 P.M., all the vans have checked in. The drivers and the other workers have gone. It is time to close the safe and call it a day.

Suddenly seven masked men walk quietly into the office. One of them holds a gun on the workers. The others tie their hands and feet and gag them.

Seventeen minutes later, the masked men walk out with over one million dollars.

The incredible Brinks job is done. The robbers are now among the world's richest crooks. And no one has any idea who they are, where they came from, or where they have gone.

The next day, news of the robbery appeared on the front pages of newspapers across the country. Everyone agreed. The robbers had done their work well. They had left no clue—not a single fingerprint—behind them.

The FBI called it "the crime of the century." It was a "perfect crime," one agent said, "carefully thought out, carefully planned." In fact—though the agent didn't know it then—over two years had been spent planning the fifteen-minute robbery.

It had all begun quietly enough, on a winter evening in 1948. Three men had gathered in the living room of a man named Tony Pino. They were all small-time crooks. But they had big ideas. And Tony had just the job they were looking for.

"Brinks," he said. "But not the vans. We're gonna go for the safe itself."

Tony and the others had been thinking about Brinks off and on for years. But they had planned to rob only the vans. In his old car, Tony had followed dozens of Brinks vans around the streets of Boston. He knew where they went. He knew the streets they followed. He knew when they were going to pick up money, and when they were carrying money. And then, one night, he followed a Brinks van all the way back to the Northside Terminal Garage.

Tony knew that the Brinks Company had garages all over the city. This one didn't look very special. But still, he decided to look around.

The garage, he saw, took up the whole first floor. What was on the second?

Tony climbed a fence. From it, he could see into one of the rooms on the second floor. He didn't expect to see anything important. But he did. He saw the Brinks Company safe.

"It was standing wide open," he said later. "And this fella was carrying money into it."

After that, Tony couldn't think about anything else. He went back to the garage every night for the next week. He didn't try to go inside. He just watched the lights go on and off. He watched people go in and out.

The lights in the safe room stayed on the latest, Tony learned. The other offices were dark by 5:30 P.M. But the safe room didn't close down until 8:00 P.M. And every night, just after eight o'clock, three or four men left the building. The watchman didn't come by until 10:30 P.M.

One night, Tony saw that the garage door was open. The garage looked empty.

"I didn't see nobody sitting at the desk," he said later. "Bang! I duck inside quick."

A door led from the garage to a staircase. Silently, Tony opened it and went up. At the top were two metal doors. Beyond them, Tony thought, must be the offices themselves. And in one of them was the safe.

Would an alarm go off if Tony opened the metal doors? There was only one way to find out.

MONEY BAGS
DISREGARDED
BY HOLDUP MEN

*A view of the open vault at the
Brinks headquarters, where gunmen
escaped with over a million dollars.*

"I took a deep breath," Tony said later. "Then I slid the door open—bang—and slid it shut. Then I tore the hell out of there. I ran down them steps and out the door and way up the block. I sat down in the doorway."

There Tony waited. He waited to see who would come running, what alarms would ring, what lights would go on upstairs. But nothing happened. Nothing at all.

The next night, Tony was back. This time, he wore a mask made out of a paper bag.

"Just in case," he said later, "they had hidden cameras in there."

He crawled up the stairs on his hands and knees. He crawled through the sliding doors and down the hallways. He picked the locks and went into some of the offices. In one of them, he found what he wanted: the safe. It was 8 feet (2.4 m) high and 9 feet (2.7 m) wide. "It was," he said, "the most beautiful thing" he had ever seen.

"If you can see a safe face to face," he told the men in his living room, "you can crack it." And that's just what he wanted to do.

Were they interested?

They were.

Sandy Richardson, Mike Geagan, and Vinnie Gusciora joined the crew that night. Joe McGinness and Specs O'Keefe joined the next month. In all, by the time of the robbery, there would be eleven of them. Tony would always be the most excited, hardest working member of the gang. But Joe McGinness, who took charge of the money, the getaway truck, and the guns, became the "official" leader.

For the next year and a half, the gang studied the Brinks building. In groups of three and four, they crept inside at night. They took their shoes off and hung them around their necks. Then they entered the offices in silence.

The men were looking for three things. They were looking for a set of keys to the offices so they wouldn't have to pick the locks each time. They were looking for a list of customers so they would know how much money was left in the safe each night. And, most important of all, they were looking for the plans to the burglar alarm system on the safe. They had to be able to turn the alarm off if they were going to rob it.

They searched two or three times a week, week in and week out. They looked in filing cabinets, mail baskets, and desks. They looked through stacks and stacks of reports and memos.

They worked slowly. They worked carefully. They worked well. No one from the Brinks Company ever knew that the offices were being searched.

The robbers couldn't find the keys. They couldn't find the plans to the alarm system. But they did find the list of customers. It told them exactly how much money was placed in the safe each night. Everything was down in black and white, a week at a time. When they were ready, they would be able to pick a good night for the robbery, a night when the safe was full.

Summer came. The gang stopped its "visits." The days were too long. And there were too many people in the streets at night. They spent July, August, and September working on other parts of the plan. They got a van. They got guns. And they got costumes.

The costumes were Tony's idea. He was very proud of it. The men would dress the way Brinks drivers dressed, navy pea jackets and green caps. But under the caps would be rubber masks, the kind that cover the whole head. With the masks on, there would be no way to tell what any of them looked like.

In October, they went back to the garage building. But they still couldn't find the keys they wanted. So they decided to make their own. Vinnie Gusciora, Specs O'Keefe, and Joe McGinness were put in charge.

They took out the locks, one by one. They brought them to a locksmith. They waited while the locksmith made keys to fit them. Then they rushed back to the Terminal Building. They replaced the locks in the doors and walked away with the keys. No one ever guessed what was going on.

Now there was only one problem left: the alarm system. They still had not found the plans to it. It began to look as though they never would. Was there any way they could do the job without the plans?

The men talked it over for weeks. They had always thought they would enter the building in the middle of the night and open the safe by force. But now, they began to think of others ways to rob it. Suppose they went inside at 7:00 P.M.? The safe would be full. The doors would be open. And the alarm would be turned off. No one would hear them come in. No one would know they were there until it was too late. They could tie up the workers and drivers, fill up their sacks with money and go. They could be in and out in a matter of minutes.

By the beginning of January, they all agreed. The robbery would be a holdup. And they were ready.

Thomas Lloyd was the first Brinks worker to slip out of the ropes in which the robbers had tied him. He set off the alarm at 7:22 P.M.

By 7:28 P.M., the police arrived.

By 8:00 P.M., all the bridges out of Boston were sealed. The police were searching the boats in the water. And police officers were checking every railroad station, bus terminal, and airport within 50 miles (80 km) of the city.

By 10:00 P.M., there were roadblocks on

every highway in Massachusetts. Every member of the State Patrol had been alerted. So had police departments up and down the East Coast all the way to Virginia. The search for the Brinks robbers was becoming the biggest manhunt in the history of the United States. And all the while, they were right there in Boston.

The FBI entered the case. In a "big sweep" of Boston, agents picked up almost everyone who had a criminal record. They wanted to know where each of them had been on the night of January 17.

Hundreds of "known Boston criminals" were brought in. McGinness, Pino, Geagan, and O'Keefe were among them. But after they were questioned, they were all let go.

The FBI took the search around the country. Five thousand ex-criminals from Maine to California were picked up. The FBI didn't get any answers. But they kept up "the heat." Sooner or later, they thought, someone would crack.

Months passed. The gang members didn't dare touch any of the money. They didn't even take the time to count it properly. Instead, they let

McGinness hide most of it away. He cheated them and they knew it. But there was nothing they could do about it then.

Most of the crooks lived quietly and worked at their regular jobs. But from time to time, some of them pulled small robberies. Tony Pino held up a small store. Mike Geagan took to shoplifting. Vinnie Gusciora and Specs O'Keefe held up an Army-Navy store near Pittsburgh, Pennsylvania. And they were caught. Gus was given five to twenty-five years for robbery. Specs was given three years on a gun charge to be followed by five to twenty-five years for the robbery itself. Though no one knew it at the time, that was the beginning of the end for the Brinks robbers.

Another year passed, and another. It was almost five years since the now-famous Brinks job. People began to believe that the robbers would never be found. Many FBI agents agreed. They were no closer to solving the case than they had been four and one-half years earlier. And soon, they knew, the "statute of limitations" would run out. According to the statute, after six years, a robbery case must be closed. Police cannot work on

it anymore. The crooks are safe. Even if they confess, they cannot be arrested. Now there was only
a year or so to go before the statute ran out on the
Brinks job. When it did, the robbers would be in
the clear.

It was at just this time that Specs O'Keefe, in
prison in Pennsylvania, began to crack. He felt
as if he would die if he had to remain in jail. He
couldn't eat. He couldn't sleep. He brooded.

Specs was almost finished with the three-
year gun charge. But then he would have to go
on trial for robbery. That meant another five years
in jail, at least. He would not be able to stand it.
He had to get out—but how?

There was one way, Specs knew. He could

*Joseph (Specs) O'Keefe is
led from the courtroom
after pleading guilty to
armed robbery. Had it
not been for his testimony,
the Brinks robbery might
never have been solved.*

offer a deal to the FBI. He was sure they would do anything he asked if he told them who the Brinks robbers really were.

Specs thought about it again and again. But he couldn't bring himself to do it. He couldn't "rat" on the gang. He was sick and he was miserable. But it would take even more to push him over the line and into the arms of the law. Then, "even more" happened.

Specs was let out on parole for the last three months of the gun sentence. He went back to Boston to get ready for the robbery trial. He wanted to hire the best lawyer he could find.

He asked McGinness for the money he would need. But McGinness turned him down.

Specs insisted.

McGinness threw him out.

That was bad enough, but McGinness went further. He hired someone to kill Specs.

The killer failed, and Specs went into hiding. When he did not report to his parole officer, the police began a search for him. He was found two weeks later and sent back to prison.

Specs wrote to McGinness one more time. He said he would forget what had happened if McGinness would come through with the money.

No one answered his letter. No one came to see him.

Specs held back until the last minute. Then, with only nine days to go on the statute of limitations, he sent for the FBI.

"What do you want to know?" he said to Special Agent Edward J. Powers. "What do you want to know about the Brinks robbery?"

"Everything," Powers answered.

And that's just what Specs O'Keefe told him.

Soon after O'Keefe's confession, all the Brinks robbers were behind bars. They had stolen $1,250,000. The government had spent almost $29,000,000 to catch them. But in the end, the "perfect crime" was solved.

INDEX